G. L. Parmelee

A Summer's Cruise in the Yacht »Swordfish«

Auxiliary Yawl

G. L. Parmelee

A Summer's Cruise in the Yacht »Swordfish«

Auxiliary Yawl

ISBN/EAN: 9783954273515
Erscheinungsjahr: 2013
Erscheinungsort: Bremen, Deutschland

© maritimepress in Europäischer Hochschulverlag GmbH & Co. KG, Fahrenheitstr. 1, 28359 Bremen. Alle Rechte beim Verlag und bei den jeweiligen Lizenzgebern.

www.maritimepress.de | office@maritimepress.de

Bei diesem Titel handelt es sich um den Nachdruck eines historischen, lange vergriffenen Buches. Da elektronische Druckvorlagen für diese Titel nicht existieren, musste auf alte Vorlagen zurückgegriffen werden. Hieraus zwangsläufig resultierende Qualitätsverluste bitten wir zu entschuldigen.

A Summer's Cruise

IN THE

Yacht "Swordfish," Auxiliary Yawl.

AS RELATED BY

The Skipper, G. L. PARMELEE,

Being a Composite Narrative of the Events of About Thirty Years, Chronicled in Many Logs.

BOSTON, 1911.

PREFACE

In writing up this little yarn, the skipper hopes it may prove as interesting to those who read it, as it has to him in recalling the many events and incidents.

The happenings of many years are chronicled in it; some of the memories are sad, some of them joyful, some funny, and some strenuous; all of them are from the logs of many cruises, and the story seems to have taken on much of the abruptness of a log, but had it been otherwise, it would have spun out to a great length, and I fear, have become monotonous. As it is I feel constrained to apologize for the many defects in it and to ask the reader's kind consideration of the fact that compiling the various small particles making up the whole story was no small task and took much more time than was anticipated.

In closing, let me dedicate this little book to the many good chums of both sexes, who have sailed with me, and who have put much of pleasure into my life. May they reap in full measure the good they have sown.

Spring Opening.

CRUISE OF THE "SWORDFISH."

IT had been the dream of the skipper, for a great many years, to be able to spend a substantial part of the Summer continuously afloat, and inclination had chosen the Coast of Maine. About every veteran yachtsman, with deep sea tendencies, gets an attack of cruisitis when the weather becomes hot, and most of them can recall plenty of disappointed plans at the last moment.

In marked contrast are the many summers when delightful two weeks cruises with good companions have been successfully brought off. Having in mind the many times that plans had fallen flat, the skipper had altered the Swordfish to a yawl, also having installed a two-cylinder engine which would give a speed of 7 miles under power, thus making a practical single hander. The dimensions of the boat may prove of interest. Over all length is 32 feet, water line 25 feet, beam 9 feet, draught 6 feet, ballast of lead between 4 and 5 tons, all outside, (making her absolutely non-capsizable). Tank for water 60 gallons, tank for gasoline, 25 gallons, (sufficient to last 3 days). The yawl rig and engine had been the work and thought of two winters. A new crowned cabin had also been added, and the top of cabin and the deck had been newly covered in the most painstaking way by laying the canvas in crude turpentine (this was later proven a great comfort).

With the above improvements it didn't seem as if any absolute defeat of plans for the summer could result.

On the 22nd of February, therefore, (the skipper being a cold air bird) the old clothes were dug up,—that venerable relic, the blue flannel shirt, with one elbow out and part of the tail missing, (surreptitiously swiped to wipe away a slip in painting), also the pantaloons, more variegated in color than ever Joseph's coat dared to be— several buttons missing and one rope suspender; who can look over these things without pleasurable anticipation of being just as darn dirty and careless of appearances as he likes. Each old paint spot can tell a story of its own, each missing button is a reminder of strenuous times. These and other articles of clothing had all been repaired and packed into the grips—those old grips which had carried tons of stuff every season when we had commenced "to go over to the boat" in the Spring, and when, in the Fall, we were about to "lay her up." Every old yachtsman knows the feeling of anticipation, the pleasure of planning, making things fit, and inventing things handy and slick looking, the putting on of paint so that it looks as good or better than that of others, and the various other things too numerous to mention.

All these things, most of them trades in themselves, and the knowledge of which comes only from years of experience, had to be done every Spring.

This year was a repetition of others, but ever new with enjoyment, and on the 22nd of February, the skipper's opening day, the procession started for the boat, determined to leave nothing undone, either of large or small importance, to add to our comfort for the Summer.

Scraping off the varnish is of course the first thing, and even although the temperature is 10 below, we are soon in a glow. Hard work, you say! It is, and when you crawl home with the last expiring ray of light, dosen't that supper taste good, and soon after you undress and fall into bed, doesn't it feel good and don't you sleep after being out in the wind, and the next morning you get up, some lame maybe but feeling like a fighting cock, and you wish, if it's Monday morning, that your job was in—well, Haverhill, so you could go over and do it some more?

The skipper's friends say he likes hard work. Well, in order to get your money's worth, you have to like it, for there is as much hard work as pleasure in yachting.

From Feb 22 till April 19,—the skipper's launching day—goes mighty quick, and if you are not careful, a good many things will go undone.

This year, the boat was hauled down on the beach Saturday, April 14, to await the coming of the tide Sunday morning.

Everybody worked till dark on the rigging, and after dark until midnight on the engine. At 3.30 a. m., Sunday morning, we turned out to find it blowing from the S. W. The line on the cradle was cast off, and the yacht slid into the water.

We immediately started the engine to run around to the mooring, but the minute the propellor was thrown on, she stopped, and, being dark, the trouble did not show by lantern.

"Well," says the skipper, "this is a good chance to try our new yawl rig." Setting jib and jigger, the anchor was hauled up and we filled away. It was blowing hard, and the skipper had some doubt about her tacking, and before getting into narrow quarters thought it advisable to try her, finding, however, that with a little coaxing she would do it. E. Boston was soon reached and we tied up to our mooring, furled up, and were soon putting ourselves outside of a good breakfast and hot coffee, which we thought we had abundantly earned. The day proved stormy, so we loafed, smoked and slept, between whiles listening to the rain on the deck. Later we installed our dynamo and storage battery, and also wired up for lights.

After tuning up the yacht for a couple of months, during which we laid plans that would have taken about 1000 years to fill. However we got everything of importance in shape by July 1. The compass, however, which had been affected by the closeness of the engine and exhaust pipe, we had to allow for, and had to swing her around the compass, making a corrected card.

We had gone aboard the night before July 1, with everything stored, tanks filled, and generously supplied with iced and solid goods.

As this is to be a voyage of pleasure and not hard work, we awoke the morning of July 1, about 7, to find a good west wind blowing. About 9, after a good breakfast, we got under way, everybody feeling fine. The crew consisted of Paul S., Martin T., who were to go the limit, also Charles C., who was to spend two weeks with us. There were others to meet us at various places on the trip.

After passing out through Shirley Gut we started sheets and had a glorious run to Gloucester. The day was cool and invigorating, quite a contrast to last year, when we ran out into an easterly and bounced about pretty much all day in a nasty sea, beating until we reached Marblehead and got among the islands, when we found smoother water under the lee of the North Shore, and made the run to Gloucester.

We reached Gloucester early this year, and had plenty of time to snug up before supper, after which we had a concert by the ship's band and singing by the quartet. A splendid evening but cold early, so the crew is willing to go to bed.

The next morning was a repetition of yesterday's weather, the wind being from the N. W.

One of the crew, nosing around for mackerel, ran across some light-salted pollock, which were mighty nice. We also bought some small mackerel from a boat coming alongside. "How much," says the Purser? "I generally gets a cent apiece," says he. Most anyone would notice from this that the fish trust hadn't got fairly started.

The wind being light, we got under way with the motor and ran out around the breakwater, which had then been completed after a number of years work by the government. At the present time most people have forgotten the havoc a south-easterly gale used to work in the outer harbor,—vessels laying at anchor there being driven ashore or against the wharves and wrecked. the breakwater off Cape Ann also furnishes a lee for vessels hard pressed and unable to make harbor. This immense work was accomplished by the government, in its usual slow, painstaking way, by dumping blocks of granite from shoal to shoal until now the rocks show at low tide. At the present time a capping of set masonry is being put on.

After running through between Milk Id. and the mainland, we found the wind had shifted to N.E., later breezing up. We set sail and were soon having a thrash to windward and bucking a head sea. Later in the afternoon, as conditions were unfavorable for Isles of Shoals or Portsmouth, we decided to run into Newburyport as being decidedly surer. The bar at the mouth of Newburyport River is constantly changing and it is well to hug the north jetty pretty close, following along the north beach fairly close, as the tide keeps this scoured out. As we wanted to get out fairly early in the morning and did not want to buck the tide, which runs pretty strong, we dropped anchor in behind the first beacon. After getting things snug we went ashore and watched them catching bait, and they certainly made some great catches. A large boat, either a row boat or power dory nosed ashore, and then began to pay out the net from the stern, letting it drift down the river, a lot of men in the water guiding and hauling it down a number of hundred feet, when the ends were hauled ashore and the net gradually gathered into a small pool, when the fish became evident, jumping and splashing in their efforts to escape. They were then baled out into boats, which soon carried them outside to waiting Cape Ann fishermen.

After the fishing was over we went aboard and had supper. In the night it came on to blow and later thundered and lightened. Some time towards morning the skipper woke up, feeling that something was wrong, and going on deck found that the boat had drifted. Threw over the big anchor and went below again.

The next morning dawned bright and clear but blowing hard from N. W. We pulled up the big anchor and started to get up sail when we found we were drifting. Hustled up jib and jigger, barely clearing the rock when we filled away. On examining things we found some lovely joker had pulled up our small anchor and put three half hitches on it. The skipper had noticed the voices of men in a boat when he got up, and supposes them to be the humorous individuals. Let us remark that it might not have looked so all-fired humorous had he caught them at it.

Having the wind fair we hustled out of the river pretty fast, and on getting outside found it blowing much harder than we had expected, accompanied by a long swell from the east. However, we made good weather of it under jib and jigger, which was plenty sufficient for sail.

The chef had been busy and now handed up to the skipper some ham and eggs and a cup of hot coffee. Maybe the breakfast didn't look good. The flying spray didn't hurt the ham and eggs very much, but mixed with coffee, is not a success.

Thick shirts and oilers were the order of the day and they felt pretty comfortable. We skirted pretty closely along the shore, which is sandy and not very interesting. Passed Portsmouth and Kittery, anchoring about 4 o'clock in the mouth of York River, running up later under power. Got in some ice and supplies before supper, properly reinforcing the supper.

We took a ride up to York Beach in the evening, finding it pretty cold. We bowled a few strings, the skipper coming out strong on the little end. Arrived back at boat about 11, and found three blankets pretty comfortable.

The next morning proved fine, and the skipper called for a vote of crew as to sailing or being lazy and exploring river. Unanimous vote for exploration, so along about 11 o'clock, the tide running in strong, we took a lunch, and getting into the tender, floated up stream. There are numerous brick yards here, the bricks turned out appearing of inferior quality. They are loaded on to barges lying alongside and towed to Portsmouth.

Landing above the brick yards, we soon had a large lot of fine huckleberries. Getting back to the tender, finally, we drifted further upstream. This river is very pretty, being quite popular with canoeists. It is about 10 miles long. Getting up pretty near the source, we found it winding about so much we were afraid of being left high and dry, so after having our lunch, we came down river. The current runs probably 4 miles an hour in the lower part of the river and possibly 3 in the upper, so that by timing it right one can have easy work both ways.

There are many fine residences on the river, owned by wealthy people, and occasionally a clubhouse is seen through the trees, automobiles coming and going; there are also a number of boathouses on the river. The banks of the river are pretty well lined with trees, making many shady little nooks which are very inviting on a hot day; this is succeeded, maybe by an occasional sweep of meadow, backed in the distance by high woodland; once in a while the rocks rise sheer from the water as though inviting a plunge into the deep water at their base. We arrived back at the boat about 5 o'clock, with good husky appetites for supper, and a thirst, which was immediately attended to by the purser. We set the table in the standing room and idled and talked over it for an hour; after clearing away the wreck we lit our pipes.

"Skipper," said Paul, "tell us about some of the trips you've made."

"Well," said the skipper, "I'll tell you as much as I can of a trip we made some years ago, I think in 1899."

"There had been two years that we had tried to get the crowd together, failing because their vacations didn't come right or something else happening at the last moment,—no yachtsman is ever sure of his cruise until the last man is aboard and you get under way. The cruise I speak of was no exception, and when it really happened I could hardly believe it. However, everybody seemed in earnest, and each one pitched in to do things for a comfortable good time. I remember Billy Macfarlane, a practical chap, got a lot of things that nobody else thought of. Cyrus Tracy,— Commodore, as we called him, since crossed over,— was a fund of dry humor that kept us on the laugh. Friend Dick, quiet and receptive, was an able assistant in starting the Commodore. Cadigan, not so well known to me, afterwards proved a mighty good cook. Well, as I said, after a couple of years trying, we got the crowd together and finally got away. On the night befor sailing Dick and myself did not get aboard till the romantic hour of 2 a. m. Sunday morning, and both of us beastly sober at that. The rest of the boys had got the things aboard and had them stowed."

"The boat had been previously hauled out and the bottom cleaned, water tanks filled, new ground tackle bent and everything looked after, for in those days the Swordfish carried some sail in her sloop rig, and the strain on blocks and rigging meant something. We had laid in a plentiful supply of beer, and very little hard stuff."

A LAZY DAY.

"Sunday morning we were up at 7 and got under way after breakfast, about 9 o'clock, I think. We went out Broad Sound, the wind being very light. The day was hot and the fellows like a lot of kids just out of school. I remember that the beer began to go so fast that Friend Dick wished we had laid in some more, but I reassured him, as most days are quite cool on the water and are not thirst producers. We arrived in Gloucester about 5 o'clock and after having supper. we chinned until 9 o'clock when we turned in."

"In those days if we wished to make any sort of a run we had to get up early, and sail late, oftentimes, consequently the next morning at 4 o'clock, I yelled 'All hands on deck;' well. talk about growling. It was the sorest crowd that I ever saw. However, they crawled out and set sail, and Cadigan, now duly elected cook, got busy, and by the time Eastern Point light was reached, (there was no breakwater then) he had a breakfast of Lyonaise potatoes, and ham and eggs, that we all did justice to. The wind was very light, and we drifted slowly, along—so slowly, in fact, that it was 11 o'clock when we passed the 'Londoner,' off Thatcher's Island."

"By this time we had set the club topsail and jib topsail. Our course, as I remember it, was about N.E. and everything was drawing in a light air, which would become a good breeze, at times, so that we would think that the topsails would have to come in, but the wind would eventually lighten up again. Thus we sailed all day, sometimes on an even keel and sometimes with rail just awash, making anywhere from 4 to 7 knots."

"We passed so far to the eastward of the Isles of Shoals that we failed to sight them at all, but we did see Mt. Monadnack. I believe the mountain, which is about 3500 feet, is situated about 60 miles inland. It is a landmark for sailors and can be seen 30 miles at sea on clear days. It is somewhat remarkable from the fact that 30 lakes can be seen from its summit."

"The sea was smooth and the day comfortably warm. Had a good hot supper at 7.30. Along towards evening the conditions were so good that we kept everything on. The moon rose early, and it was one of the most beautiful nights I ever saw,—light as day. The boat was so evenly balanced that the tiller was amidship in the comb and I don't think it was moved all night. Everybody was loth to go to bed, but as we were running all night, watches had to be stood, so Dick and I, having the last watch, turned in for a few winks."

"Along about 12 o'clock, Cadigan made some coffee and sandwiches for us, and Dick and I climbed into our overcoats, for it had grown chilly, and were left to our fate."

"I remember, along toward 4 o'clock we began to look for lights, and thought we saw them, but probably didn't. However, between 5 and 6 we saw the coast line. In the meantime our noted chef had got in his work and soon set a breakfast before us that tasted mighty good."

"After breakfast Billy got out the chart and finally declared that two white points on the horizon were Matinicus Rock. I remember I didn't think it was possible we had made so much easterly or footed so fast. However, later sight proved the correctness of his eye-sight, and, as I think of it even now, I have to give the boat a large credit mark for a wonderful performance. We made Carver's Harbor at 2 o'clock, 27 hours from the 'Londoner,' a distance of 175 miles, averaging about 6¼ knots per hour. About an hour after making port it commenced to rain and turned foggy, which lasted three days. We spread an old sail over the cockpit and listened with a good deal of comfort to the gusts of wind and patter of rain on the cabin top. Some of the boys played cards till supper time, while the rest of us sat around and smoked and talked."

"The next day we went ashore and looked over the town and quarries, where they get out some very fine granite. We saw a piece which we measured and found to be 65 feet long. They also had a stone turning mill similar in appearance to a wood turning machine. We were told they did considerable fancy work with it. The mill took fire the last night of our stay and burnt completely down. Carver's Harbor is on the south side of Vinal Haven, which forms part of the right shore of Penobscot Bay."

"Here a few yawns from the audience brought the yarn to an abrupt close."

The next morning we were awakened by the toots of a tug bringing a tow of brick barges down the river. It was rather interesting to see the tug swing those big barges so close to shore, especially in the narrows below us which are no wider hardly than a country brook.

The weather was fine, with a good breeze from the N. W. After breakfast we got under way with power, running out of the river, then setting sail. The wind which had been good, lightened up, and we drifted lazily along. Toddy, with rifle, is shooting everything in sight and some things not in sight. Paul is joking Toddy, and trying to act as though he were enjoying himself.

We drifted along until about 1 o'clock and as the

wind is light, and the clouds show some promise of a squall, the harbor of Cape Porpoise looks good to us. This harbor is made up of islands and shoals between them leaving only a narrow rocky entrance opening to the sea. Originally a shoal small harbor, it has been improved by the government until it is now a fair-sized deep harbor, if care is taken to avoid the flats. We ran up to head of harbor and picked up a mooring. Had dinner and then went ashore on the islands, which are quite pretty, and on which there are a good many berries in their season. The outer shore of the island on the north is rocky, with a narrow beach of large bowlders, torn from the parent rock by the heavy seas of Winter. The harbor side is sandy or marshy, with broad, sandy flats. The tide was out when we rowed back to the yacht.

The boys started back, however, to investigate some crabs they had seen and also to dig some clams. They were armed with the fire shovel and pails.

The skipper was busy about some little job on the boat, when his attention was attracted by a yell. Looking up he saw Toddy bat a crab to Paul, who side swiped it back to Toddy. Well, Toddy chased it into the air as far as he could reach, and when that crab started back for the beach, Paul made more hieroglypic motions to head him off than were ever discovered in Egypt. Well, finally they winded the crab and landed him in the pail, and Paul solemnly swears that if he hadn't broken the crab's right wing they would never have got him. Finally, by dint of much sprinting, they got a pailfull, and then turning their attention to the clams, dug a pailful of those. The clams were a little small but were very white, and after feeding them meal for a couple of days, were fine eating.

Well, we had for supper, hot biscuit, clam bouillion, steamed clams and crab stew. The crab stew attracte the particular attention of the boys. "By gosh, skipper," says Toddy," that stew is bully, what did you put in it?"

"I am not giving away my cooking recipes," said the skipper, "I learnt how to make a stew from the noted French chef, Monsieur Hutch "

"Well, Monsieur Hutch and you are both it," says Paul, as he finished the last of about two gallons.

After supper, everybody seemed to have an inclination to loaf, or at least until later when the outrigger of the jigger called for considerable attention.

"The first time I ever made this harbor," said the skipper, "was in 1905, I think. We started from the Isles of Shoals about 9 in the morning, and ran to Appledore Island to get some ice. It looked like a good day and we were going to try and make Portland. About an hour, however, after leaving the shoals the fog set in mighty thick. That was the first year with the engine in the boat. The iron exhaust from the engine ran so near the compass that it could not be corrected, and all we could do was to make an allowance card. Our course was nearly or quite north, and that seemed to be the sensitive point of the needle. I had that strongly impressed on my memory. As I said, our course was north. Now if the yacht's course was altered ever so little to the east the needle would begin to fly to east by north, and if it varied at all to the west it would fly to west by north, so you can imagine it required some close watching."

"Well, one of the boys with me wanted to take the tiller and I let him. Five minutes were enough for him.

"Here, skipper," he says, "you take this damned thing, I can't keep her anywhere.

"I didn't blame him much, as when the needle was describing quarter circles each side of North it was mighty disconcerting, but this very fact was in favor of a straight correct course, as the least bit of deviation brought you up with a jerk. When the fog had set in we had paid out the log, estimating the distance already run, and, as I had made up my mind not to run all day in the fog if I could help it, I determined to try for Cape Porpoise, especially as our course took us close by there. The time seemed pretty long running in the fog. but we finally ran off our distance and wound in the log, We ran, perhaps, fifteen minutes longer, and I had begun to think we had run by when we heard the bell buoy off the entrance to the harbor, and in another minute saw it directly ahead of our bowsprit; we let her off and ran in, the closeness of the rocks looking mighty scary. When we got fairly inside, we nearly ran down a dory with a man asleep in it. He piloted us up the harbor and put us on a buoy. You can be sure we felt pretty comfortable to get in. Later when the fog lifted for a few minutes we saw a large sloop outside which had got into a pocket and had to drop her anchor."

"That summer there was a good deal of fog and we were stalled here a couple of days."

"A small sloop with a man, his wife and a boy came in later. He was light draft, however, and had followed the shore. It is quite a saying with yachtsmen that coming from the west, one could never find the harbor, but now they have got a whistler some distance off the harbor and I think it could be made. Another fine day. After breakfast we got under way; wind light and we are drifting slowly along. The day is hot and later on our lunch and iced beer tastes pretty good. Paul was the purser, today, and say, he is a generous cuss. His idea of a sandwich is to make it thick. The skipper's was so thick he had to yell for a marline spike to pry his jaws open far enough to span it. Toddy is trying to give the gulls on the buoys hot feet with his rifle. Everything considered, we are passing a fairly successful day. The wind dying out later, we started the power and ran into Peak's Island. After supper, we went ashore.

We usually spend a couple of days in Portland, and as there are a number of things we want done, think we had better do them now. Toddy and Paul, both being from Ohio, about everything is new to them. Paul, being a practical machinist, doesn't like some sound about the engine, and as he hails from somewhere in the vicinity of Missouri, proposes to be shown. Toddy and the skipper visit the town for necessary supplies. Toddy tries to beat the pawnbrokers, with doubtful success. After going to the postoffice for mail we get our supplies and go aboard, finding Paul with a dissected engine, and looking every inch a laboring man. Had supper and went over to Peak's Island in the evening.

The next day we finished up the engine, and she certainly works better and quieter. Got in our gasoline and ice, and went out to Cape Cottage for dinner.

The skipper had always heard of the beautiful Casco Bay, but heretofore in the hurried cruises there had seemed to be no time to visit it.

The weather was somewhat uncertain the next

morning, but we determined to start, so as soon as breakfast was cleared away we started under power. setting sail after getting under way. Passed out of the harbor on the North side of Peak's Island, and had a very pretty sail among the islands, passing Long Island and the Little Chebeag, through Chandler's Cove by Great Chebeag, Hope Island, Stave Island, and a number of small islands, finally running into Pott's Harbor about 4 o'clock, and we got our anchor down and furled up just in time to escape a squall which had been chasing us up.

This is a harbor well protected by small islands and shoals, and has a good soft bottom on the North side. It is said there are about 1000 islands in Casco Bay and that you can drop anchor anywhere in the bay and be well protected. Pott's Harbor is one of the usual summer boarding places, of which there are a good number, every island of any size probably bidding for the city folks. All of these islands are visited by the steamers of the Casco Bay line, bringing them in close connection with each other and also with Portland.

The next morning proving fine we ran over to town for ice, and then went out the south channel under power. This channel is narrow, hardly wide enough for sail. Ran to bell buoy off Jaquish Island, from there headed for the Brown Cow, passing it on port side at some distance. Passed White Bull and Mark Islands, then running for Wood Island, thence up New Meadow River. This was recommended to us as a pretty sail, and it certainly is beautiful. Given a warm day, a light favoring wind, beautiful scenery, green trees and singing birds, the smell of the trees, who wouldn't be happy.

At least the skipper was in a dream until that practical Paul pushed a ham sandwich and a cold bottle into his fist, and, well, that wasn't so bad either. About two hours sail brought us to the head of practical navigation.

There is a cafe here noted for its fish dinners and they are certainly good. This is a warm night, and the cabin being warm we sat out in the cockpit after supper, but the mosquitoes got so fierce we couldn't stand it, so went below, after adjusting the netting; even then the mosquitoes gathered outside and barked at us.

We got up early next morning to take advantage of the tide. There being very little wind, and that little dead ahead, we ran with power until off Small Point, and then putting on sail, we drifted along and into the Kennebec River, anchoring behind the fort. After geting in sail and making everything snug, we found we had skated out into the river, and had to start motor to get back. We had anchored on a slate ledge. There is nothing of especial interest here, but a very interesting sail may be had up the river to Bath, then into the Sassanoa through a draw bridge, and the passage made to Boothbay. The Sassanoa cuts a large slice of land from the mainland, making a virtual island of it. This trip up the river and down to Boothbay was taken by the skipper a good many years ago, and is remembered as a very pretty and novel trip. The Sassanoa River is very narrow in places, in others broadening out into lake like proportions. The shores vary from bold and rocky in places to marshy and shallow in others; considerable care has to be exercised to keep in the channel. At Big Hell Gate the current at half tide is dangerous to the uninitiated. The skipper on his initial trip thought discretion the better part of valor and waited for slack water. Even then our hair stuck up some, as we were carried by the current towards one bank until we thought we were aground and then rushed by the current over to the other bank, putting out our hands to fend off from the rocks. After leaving Hell Gate, however, we sailed down the river with the last of the ebb and out into Sheepscot Bay. From here it is only a short run across the Sheepscot river and through Townsend Gut to Boothbay. Townsend Gut as well as the Sheepscot, however, are very surprising streams. Townsend Gut is narrow most of its length, and the banks of both streams are, in places, straight sheer walls, looking as though sliced down by some gigantic knife, and a sailboat, beating through here with a head wind can run its bowsprit literally ashore and into the bushes without touching bottom with the keel. Townsend Gut, like the Sassanoa, cuts off a large lot of land called Southport island, from the mainland. Boothbay is a fair harbor in most winds.

We bought a fine cod at Fort Popham for supper, after which we sat out in the cockpit until it got cold.

We were lazy the next morning as we were only making a short run. After breakfast was cleared away we started the motor and the tide helping us we were soon outside. Our course took us by Cape Newaggen and we ran in here for dinner. This is a curious little harbor, formed on the outer point of Southport Id. by three small islands, there being three narrow entrances. Like a good deal of the shore down here, you can, and in some cases must, run very close to the shore. In the case of the north entrance to this harbor you look over the side and see the rocky reef, while on the other side you might almost touch the sheer rock. It is a nice quiet harbor, however, with plenty of water when once inside. The easterly entrance is a crooked rather shallow entrance. The middle channel has rocks in the middle of it. Southport Island is a pretty, well wooded island, 6 miles long, perhaps, and is connected to the mainland at Boothbay by a drawbridge. After dinner, we motored out of the harbor and pointed for Boston Island.

The skipper has a friend there who keeps a hotel, and he had been invited for many years to visit him, which he had steadily neglected to do. This year however, having plenty of time, it seemed a good chance to reap the many promises of a good time. Consequently, after a short uneventful run, we dropped the hook, and with shore togs on proceeded to look him up. Now they say all hotel keepers are royal good fellows; be that as it may, however, we were royally greeted both by him and his wife, both of them old friends of long standing, and nothing would do but we must stay to supper. Well, shore meals are not to be despised, especialy with good friends. Sitting on the piazza, after supper, and recalling incidents of thirty years ago, some of them almost forgotten, is pleasant to most of us and was certainly so to the skipper. We took leave about 9 o'clock, after leaving an invitation for them to sail with us and bring anyone they saw fit. Getting back to the boat we consulted the ice chest, had a smoke and turned in. The boys were up early in the morning to prepare for visitors washing down the deck and scrubbing the seats, crockery, etc.

Along about 10 o'clock, our visitors arrived and we

A Happy Bunch

got up sail and stood out to sea. Now it wasn't long before the party got acquainted. The women, of course, had to see how the men managed their house, how they cooked, and were variously inquisitive about everything. Now a yachting party with the weather pleasant, not too much breeze, sea smooth, is one of the delightful things of life, especially if there are pretty girls in the crowd,— ask Toddy and Paul if it is not so. Later in the day we dropped anchor close to a small island, and going ashore built a fire to make coffee. Toddy and Paul gathering the wood, with the kind assistance of some of the girls. The wood didn't seem to come in very fast, so the skipper had to gather a little himself, noticing at the same time that the boys seemed more busy at gathering feminine fingers.

Finally the table was set, a white table cloth having been produced from somewhere, and more dainty fragrant grub on the table cloth than would sink a ship. Well it was good, with the accent on the good, and about all the young people mixed it with a lot of giggles, and the skipper, well, confound it, you wouldn't exactly call his cachinations giggles, but, anyhow, he made some noise, that is, until a sweet young thing of some 60 summers, or winters, nobody knows which, asked him if he was married. Now wouldn't that embarrass any well brought up skipper.

It didn't seem as if we were at lunch very long, but the sun seemed to be getting heavy in the west, and we bundled the party aboard as fast as we could, which wasn't so very darn fast either.

The wind having dropped, we started the motor and pointed towards our starting point. By this time everybody was as well aquainted as any old friends of a few hours can be; there wasn't a single idle moment, and you can bet there wasn't a still one. Boston Id. was reached all to soon, and our party went ashore leaving an invitation for the ship's crew to a dance in the evening. The boys were rather backward about going with their ordinary clothes, but the skipper reassured them, quoting with the wisdom of an oracle, "You go; if any Willie shows up in evening clothes, your brown mugs will win," and the skipper noticed in looking on that his words were as those of a prophet. Now, the skipper can't remember whether it was very late or very early when we went aboard, but that is immaterial for there's no doubt everybody had a good time.

Early in the morning the skipper's friend, Bert, was alongside with an invitation to a trip in his launch, so after breakfast we went ashore and later were taken through to Boothbay and back, then up the Sassanoa River, recalling many old landmarks partly forgotton by the skipper, all of the trip especially interesting to the boys, however; that is, in their idle moments,—for the girls had to be looked after, you know.

We arrived back at the island about 2 o'clock, and our friends fairly kidnapped us for lunch, not that kidnapping was necessary, but you know how it is, gentle reader, you have to pretend you have important business, when you know it is a damn lie, and everybody else knows it; now why is it,— somebody please furnish the answer.

Along about 4 o'clock, we went aboard to fix up a little, as we had invited our friends aboard for the evening, as we were sailing on the next day. Like real nice housekeepers the boys tidied up the cabin, slicked up the standing room, made Flemish coils of the ropes, etc.

put plenty of stuff on the ice, and last, but not least, attended to their personal adornment, the skipper arranging some lights for the standing room, connecting to the battery. Now these lights were not search lights, not by any means; they were just those cute pretty little things that showed some light in the immediate vicinity very immediate, leaving plenty of dim places forward, much dimmer by comparison.

Along about seven o'clock our party arrived, and in about five minutes there were bunches of chatter distributed all over the boat. Bert and his wife were much interested to look over the battery, dynamo, etc., rather wondering at the number of conveniences for the size of boat, and we sat in the cabin for a few minutes recalling some of our experiences as shipmates years ago, finally reaching the standing room. By this time the shadows had taken positions closely reminding one of a matrimonial agency and that recalls the fact that many couples, in the skipper's remembrance, have met on the Swordfish, finally putting on double harness. There is something fasinating about a quiet night on the water, moonlight or otherwise, and with a nice girl that you are a little mushy on the result is almost certain. Try it girls. As the skipper looks back and thinks of the many friends who have sailed with him, in the many years of his yachting experience, a good many memories are recalled.

Some have long since gone to their reward; of those remaining many who are mated have passed through much trouble, the great destroyer having claimed their mates, while others having passed through trouble are now looking ahead to a life of peace; and still others are being tried by fire,— who can understand it. All we know is that it makes us feel solemn, sad, glad, or sympathetic.

However, sad thoughts can't last long with this party of which a number are good singers and are proving it. Can you beat it. A bunch of happy people mostly young, laughing, singing, making love and enjoying themselves. Just now a boat came alongside bringing ice cream and cake — our thoughtful friend again. Refreshments being served, more singing is the order,— and the evening getting late our guests begin to depart.

Our friend suggested that if the next day proves fair he will take a run part way with us, and we suggest making our plans to reach Christmas Cove, taking part of party with us.

On the departure of the last load of our party, the boys lit their pipes and leaning back in the cockpit voiced their sentiment thusly: "By gosh, skipper, but we are certainly having bunches of good times," and from all appearances I should judge they were right. After a short smoke, we turned in and slept the sleep of the just, the dead tired, or anything else that is just plain tired.

The next day dawned clear and bright, and the crew were promptly on deck to wash down and clean up. While the boys were washing down, the skipper was getting breakfast, and as the smoke curled out of the stove pipe and the smell of ham and eggs circulated up the companion way, the crew made frequent excursions to the standing room to see how things were coming on. Breakfast over we proceeded to get sail on as there was a fair breeze. Promptly at nine o'clock our friend motored up and put such of the party aboard as desired to come, and the skipper noticed two young ladies particularly desired to come. Says he to himself, "by the the great wall knot, but it is lucky I'm getting away from here, or I'd lose my crew." Sailing lazily along we enjoyed the soft sea breeze to the utmost, the boys especially, as it is their last day with the ladies. After awhile, Bert steamed alongside and suggested lunch at Newaggen which struck us properly, so along about noon we ran in and laying the boats alongside enjoyed lunch together. After lunch, the boys suggested a run ashore. The road leading to Boothbay is through trees about all the way and a walk along this is delightful, and undoubtedly so with the present company. Now all good things come to an end and three o'clock suggests time to get away. Going aboard our friend tows us out of the harbor and we bid them all good bye with a good deal of reluctance and promises all round to look them up at home. The breeze petered out about four o'clock, so we started up the motor and ran to Christmas Cove for the night. The shores along here are very pretty, being bold and rocky and for the most part they are well occupied by cottages. Entering the Damariscotta River, it is a short run of two miles to Christmas Cove. The shores of this river are a continuation of the beautiful scenery. We arrived in the cove early in the afternoon and making everything snug for the night, had supper and went ashore. There is a large hotel here which seems pretty well patronized, and about everybody in the place takes boarders in the summer. An ice cream parlor, a dance hall and bowling alley seem to be well patronized; in fact outside of bathing and sailing in the party boats, that is about all to break the monotony, although many people seem to bring their own boats or canoes with them. Bowling seemed to attract our party, and Paul, to exercise himself, tried to stave holes in the wall. After a few strings we went back to the boat, the skipper fearing he would have to pay for a new building.

By vote of the crew the next day was spent here; after breakfast, the tide being low, we went ashore and dug some clams, (small, but good), and then paddled around until dinner time. We loafed over our dinner and fished the rest of the afternoon, catching a good mess which we had for supper, and they tasted mighty good. A small yacht came in this afternoon with some good voices on it, and we had quite an interesting concert in the evening, as they had a fine sounding phonograph and a goodly lot of records. Some fishing boats came in tonight and swept the bay for fish. Don't believe they were very successful. There is also a fish wier which we looked into in the afternoon. These fish wiers seem to represent a lot of work, and seem to catch very little, in fact, it looks as though the fishermen earn all they get.

Voted to spend another day here, consequently a lazy breakfast, after which a trip ashore. Walking past the hotel, one is, after a short distance, high on the rocks and looking seaward in an easterly direction. After a blow, it is quite an inspiring sight to watch the sea break over the isolated rocks lower down and dash up on the shore. Retracing our steps we are soon on a road leading inland through ordinary country scenery. After quite an extended ramble, the pangs of hunger begin to make themselves manifest, and a hasty retreat is ordered.

Arriving back at the yacht, a cold bottle and cheese or sardine sandwiches seems to put things in shape. After lunch we took the tender and explored the southeast shore. On near examination, one finds many curious little openings, due to the rotting away of the dykes or softer volcanic stone which has erupted through the granite in bygone ages. These rocks geologically, are very old, and many of the little harbors like Cape Newaggen are due to the decaying away of the softer rock which has been forced through the granite by former disturbances, leaving, in some instances, as straight and smooth a wall as though hewn. The Sassanoa and Sheepscot rivers are undoubtly due in part to this same thing. Having explored about everything of interest, we rowed back to the yacht and spent the rest of the afternoon in getting in supplies.

The next day proving fair, we ran out of the harbor with the motor, setting sail outside. It is a warm day and the sun is hot, but there is just breeze enough to make it cool and fan us lazily along.

Everybody is doing something, Toddy writing his girl, Paul singing and mending some of his things and the skipper busy with some splicing. Pemaquid Point and the light loom up further along and are passed about an hour later. Tradition has it about here that this point was settled very early in the history of this country. There is no doubt that many stirring events took place here. There is quite a museum of interesting articles near the light. Rounding Pemaquid we soon reached New Harbor, a small elongated harbor, guarded at its entrance by a reef of rocks from the north side, and a few feet further along by a reef from the south side. In an easterly blow there is quite a swell rolls in, but it is nevertheless a pretty good harbor. Bristol is strictly a fishing town and the harbor is full of fishing boats,—so full, in fact, as to afford scant anchorage to visiting craft. In the afternoon the fog rolled in and we had it for three days.

A fisherman coming in gave us some fish and they

went mighty nice for supper. The next morning after a lazy breakfast, we went ashore for a walk out to the Cape by the inland road. This is rather a pretty walk of about four miles. Visited the light and talked with the keeper. For a fog horn they have an arrangement which they wind up with a windlass, a clock arrangement releasing a weight, which forces air, every few minutes, into the whistle or horn.

For washing water they catch the rain from the roof, and although this light is well up on the rocks, we were told that the spray would at times make the water quite hard. For drinking water they had to go to the next house.

We walked back along the shore. The rocks here are like steps, interrupted occasionally by a washed out dyke. A walk over this kind of thing, although interesting, begins to be tiresome when you have covered four miles and we arrived back to the yacht with the foundation of an appetite. We got acquainted with a lobsterman who came in from his traps tonight. Invited him aboard and prescribed for his cough. Had quite an interesting chat with him. He told how he was on Monhegan Id., in the storm in which the Portland was lost, visiting aboard a fisherman, and being caught by the blow, was unable to get ashore. He said he expected to go adrift every moment, in which case all hands would have been lost. The anchor held, however, although they passed anything but a comfortable night. When our visitor left, he gave us a lot of small lobsters, and, as one of the crew expressed it, for the next two or three days we had lobster boiled, fried, a la Newburg, lobster stew, and lobster tut, tut.

Another day of fog. Went ashore after breakfast

and had a long walk. Nothing very interesting. went over to the lobster pound in the afternoon. This is a salt water pond, formed by building a dam and backing up the water. We were told that there were 30,000 lobsters in the pond. The water was so cloudy that very few lobsters were visible. This strikes the ordinary spectator as being one of those contrivances for making the price high in the winter. The pond is owned by a Portland concern, the lobsters being caught and placed in the pond during the Summer and taken out during the Winter.

Towards night the weather indications pointed to clearing weather, and we got in ice and supplies.

The next morning being fine we got under way after breakfast and had a short sail across to Friendship Id.

A friend of Toddy's was summering here in charge of the Y. M. C. A. encampment, and our friend C. that quiet chap, of which not much has been said, had his girl to find. He had been fretting some when laid up by fog only a few miles from her. It seems that the girl's folks did not take kindly to the young man's suit and were trying to break it up. Well Charlie found the young lady, but came back to the yacht in about as gloomy a state as man well could, as the young lady was being spirited away that night for a trip to Europe. To cheer him up as much as possible, the skipper proposed that they all row over early so that Charlie might see as much as possible of her before the steamer left, and after a hasty bite we left. A few minutes before the boat was to leave Charlie came down looking pretty bad. He got into the tender and sat down. Nobody felt like intruding on his thoughts so we just shoved off into the twilight and drifted. Finally

Charlie picked up his guitar, which somebody had put into the boat and began to sing. He had a fine voice and when he finally sung: "Sing au revoir, but not good bye," well the feeling that he put into that song affected all of us, and I was told afterwards that the young lady broke down completely. So that the reader may not be left in suspense the skipper interpolates that everything came right with the young people later; Charlie was a very quiet chap, but devilish persistent and as he steadily made good in his business he finally won over the hard hearted parents.

Well it was rather a subdued party that rowed back to the yacht, where we found Thomas waiting for us.

This is a pretty spot, rather full of unsuspected shoals, however, and only a careful following of the chart will keep one out of trouble.

Next morning was bright, with no wind; used the motor, running around through Port Clyde. After leaving Port Clyde we set sail with a light breeze, running slowly to Whitehead Light, where the breeze freshened, and we ran across Penobscot Bay with all the wind we needed and a little more. Toddy took another of his freak photos, going aloft to the masthead to do it, and with his usual skill got a successful picture where no result might have been expected. We arrived at North Haven about 2 o'clock. Bought some supplies here,—mighty little, however, as prices are pretty high.

After getting things aboard we ran over to Perry's Cove, which used to be called by the skipper. "The quietest place on Earth."

There is a little island in the mouth of this cove, and it looked so inviting to the boys that they wanted to camp out. So we took the awning and made a windshield with it in a clump of trees, then placing the cushions under it pulled a log up to rest our feet on and built a fire in front of it. Then, rolling up in our blankets, we were mighty cozy.

Next day was a nice clear day. After breakfast we rowed up to the head of the cove which is a mile or more long. This cove seems to be another of those queer formations we find down this coast; it looks like a river, but is simply quite a pretty inlet.

The land here is being rapidly taken up for cottages and what was formerly. "The quietest place on Earth," now begins to echo to the patter of the motor boat.

In the afternoon we gathered some mussels which we had for supper, along with hot biscuits.

This morning we decided to go along, and after breakfast, we set sail for Deer Island Thoroughfare. This course takes us all the way among a lot of islands and shoals,—as picturesque a bit of scenery, probably, as there is anywhere on the coast; indeed, Penobscot Bay has often been called the "Naples of America." Yachtsmen are not given to hysterics over scenery, but as I once heard one of them say, "a sail among beautiful islands or up a river where the birds are singing and you have the smell of pine trees, is my idea of a good time," and, we might add, that the sight of the mighty swell of the ocean on barren ledges distant from the shore works a mysterious fascination on the mind. There is certainly plenty of food for all of these feelings along this part of the coast.

Passing out of Deer Id. Thoroughfare we ran across to Casco Passage and tied up for the night. After an early supper, a lazy evening in the cockpit is not out of place, and after pipes are lighted, the skipper is reminded of his unfinished yarn.

"I believe we left off where we were just leaving Carver's Harbor. Carver's Harbor is on the south side or seaward side of Deer Isle, we having passed along the north side today. It is nearly as full of shoals there as it is here, and I remember we made a short cut by Merchant's Id. The day was a fine one. The wind freshened up soon after leaving the harbor and we had to take in the topsails which we had previously set, but, as the wind died down again, we reset the light sails and drifted slowly along towards Bass Point. The day was hot and the wind fluky. The scenery of Mt. Dessert is pretty and impressive, some of the numerous elevations extending clear to the coast. Everybody felt happy and the iced beer was not at all bad. After passing Bass Harbor we took in the balloon jib, and a little later the club-topsail, as we got more wind than we wanted, but the breeze soon died out and left us drifting 5 miles from Bar Harbor. After waiting awhile we commenced to tow and finally anchored at 10.30. All hands were mighty tired and cranky. We staid there two days, one an account of stormy weather and one for visiting, all hands going up the mountain.

As our time was getting short we turned out the next morning at three o'clock, finding it a beautiful day. I remember Billy felt pretty bad over the early rising question and sarcastically referred to our virtuous breakfast as a late supper. However, I didn't notice any feeble appetites. Off Otter Cliff, we set the topsails but later had to take them in and reef the mainsail, and we fairly lugged this sail to Casco Passage, where we shook out the reefs. The wind changed to dead ahead here and we made slow work of it to Fox Island Thoroughfare arriving early in the evening. We stood in to the town for supplies of ice, etc. I remember after getting these aboard, we left the ice in the tender, and in filling away the painter jumped over a rowlock and before we knew it the tender took a dive and broke adrift. We stood back, picking up the oars, etc. Then baling out the tender we searched for the ice, and when we found it, it was about one fourth of its original size, the rest having disappeared from the action of the salt. We stood over to Perry's Cove and anchored. After a good hot supper everybody was tired, so turned in early.

The next morning was cool and bright. There was, as usual, great enthusiasm over the early rising question, so much so I had to call in the doctor, who quickly diagnosed the ailment and quickly prescribed for it. As we had got under way before breakfast, everybody got interested in the movements of the chef, and he, not used to so much attention, began to get uneasy. However, nothing serious happened until breakfast was on the table, and for about an hour if ever there was a poor down-trodden over-worked cook, it was Cadigan. However, everything has an end. With a good breeze, we had a good quick run across to Whitehead Light, where we found a nasty head chop sea which was anything but inspiriting. Billy and I were below laying off the course when there was a crash—the topmast had gone,— owing to a faulty shackle in the port stay. Billy went aloft and we soon had the wreck on deck. We had been meaning to make the Damariscotta River, but beating in a sea is not conducive to speed, and we had to run into New Harbor for the night, arriving about 8 o'clock. I can remember that the quiet of that little harbor felt mighty good after the all day jounce.

The next day we fixed the topmast, while waiting

for breakfast, and got away about 9 o'clock. There was no wind and we towed out of the harbor; getting a light breeze about 11 o'clock, we set our course for Seguin and passed the light about 5 o'clock. The wind was light and uncertain, dying out at times and coming up again. It was 1.30 in the morning when we anchored in Portland harbor. Everyone was so tired that supper was of no consequence, and we all fell into bed. About an hour later, however, we were awakened by the fog horn on the light and had to get our tired bones together and pull the boat out of the roadway."

"Well, fellows, while that tired crew is getting a nap, suppose we do the same. It's getting chilly and I think the blankets might feel good."

The next day broke fine, but not a breath of wind, so power was the order of things most of the way to Bar Harbor. As we passed Bass Harbor it recalled the first visit the skipper made quite a number of years ago. It was sunset when we passed and it was dark when we beat up by Great Cranberry Island. It was so dark that the lookout on the bowsprit didn't see a fish wier and we almost ran into it. We finally ran into N. E. harbor or the night and anchored.

The breeze continued light, the next morning so we ran up the coast with the motor by Schooner Head and the breakwater and anchored in Bar Harbor.

The next day proving fine we went ashore and hired a buckboard to take us up the mountain. On the skipper's first visit they had a small steamer running across the lake, connecting with an inclined railway. On a very clear day, a fine view can be had from the mountain, and vessels a considerable distance at sea can be seen. Years ago there was a weather station at the top, which is now given up. There is nothing of interest to see now except the view, and there seem to be very few days when the air is clear enough to see any great distance. We were soon on our way down the mountain, arriving without special incident. We went over to Sorrento in the afternoon; this appeared to be a sleepy place; it may be intentionally so or we may not have struck it right. We arrived back about supper time. A remark from someone about the great rise and fall of the tide recalled an incident of long ago, when we had tied our tender at high tide to one of the spiles. On our return we were surprised to see the tide some 18 feet lower, and if some good fellow hadn't moved our tender for us, we'd have been obliged to get a ladder and pick it off the tree. Bar Habror is somewhat disappointing to the visiting yachtsman unless he is acquainted. It is a poor harbor during uncertain weather conditions, and one usually feels glad to get away. There is the drive across the island, which is quite pretty, however.

The next morning we left on the homeward journey, having a good breeze. It is always well to look for squalls here, as they frequently come down off the high land with great force, but we ran down the coast without incident, rounding Bass Point and running across through Casco passage. Had lunch of cheese sandwiches and cold beer, which tasted pretty good in the warm sunshine. The wind lightened up in the afternoon but we finally made North Haven (Perry's Cove) and anchored for the night.

The next morning dawned clear and after breakfast we got underway. Running along through the passage, we passed an old hooker just as we were mixing one of those iced drinks, and as the tinkle of the ice reached the ears of the old moss-back at the wheel, it was a caution to see the grin on his face, and the way he ran his tongue over the stubble on his chin was edifying to the boys. It was wicked I know to tantalize the old chap that way—it was even more—it was criminal, but it couldn't be helped. Passing out by the light, we ran about an hour when we noticed the fog settling down over the masts of a schooner. Took a compass course and were soon enveloped in thick fog. Headed for the bell buoy off Ash Island and soon had our anchor down behind the island.

It soon changed to a thick chilly mist and we started a coal fire and made ourselves comfortable. A little later the boys got uneasy and went fishing—maybe the sound of ladies' voices somewhere in the fog had something to do with it. Be that as it may however, they got a nice string of fish which we had for supper. The next day was still foggy and we slept late. Had breakfast and later went ashore and walked up to the postoffice. There is not much of interest here and we were all glad when the fog cleared away just after dinner time.

The tide was running strong against us and we were only able to make Seal Harbor. This harbor is rightly named, and we could hear the sea pigs growling and barking whenever we woke up in the night.

The next morning we got under way with sail, but on passing out by Whitehead Light found a bad sea running with considerable wind. Had hoped to make Port Clyde today but was forced to run into Tennant's Harbor. The next day being Sunday and still blowing, we decided to stay and be lazy.

A young fellow came along in a motor dory and talked with us awhile, and we later met him ashore and were invited to dinner. He said they were only going to have a lobster stew but would be glad to have to have us come. "Only going to have lobster stew," says Paul, under his breath. Well we went and found them nice everyday people who had this cottage down on the shore where they came Sundays to picnic. The boys were all a little backward, but we were put at our ease in a very few minutes, and we certainly spent a delightful day with them.

The next day was bright and warm and we started out under power. After running about an hour, the nut and part of the stem on the forward cylinder snapped off and went overboard. "Here's a joke," says the skipper. However, we set sail, working our grey matter to see what we could do with the engine. We took out the forward peep plug and disconnected the wire from that cylinder thus making a one cylinder engine. Running with one cylinder was slow work and we made about 4 knots an hour. We ran by Port Clyde, making the passage by George's Island. Later in the afternoon the wind was ahead and the remaining cylinder refused to work, but as there was a little more breeze we got along pretty well and ran into Christmass Cove about 8 o'clock.

The next morning was a perfect calm. While Paul was juggling with breakfast the skipper was shaking ice. There was a wrecking sloop in the harbor, and say, gentle reader did you ever see a horse prick up its ears when someone said oats? Did you ever try on a still hot morning, when a sound will travel miles — did you ever try shaking ice? Of course you will need other things. If you never did try it, do so, and see the people look up and begin to hang their tongues out. Well those fellows on the sloop immediately discovered an errand ashore and their course laid close by us. Of course we couldn't let them go by without saying, "good morning." Well it's astonishing what a little bit of the stuff will do along the coast; after one drink, they'd give us their shirt, and after two they'd love us like a brother. It is needless to say that we left with a cargo of lobsters.

After breakfast we got our supplies and got under way. The skipper had been rummaging around to see if something couldn't be found to doctor up the other cylinder of the engine. There were about 4 or 5 turns of thread left on the stem, and it occurred to him that if a nut could be found to fit that, with a shortened spring that cylinder might furnish a little help. A nut which was a little too large was hammered on two opposite sides until it would go on snug with a little shellac, then putting in the plug and hitching on the wire, we gave the fly wheel a whirl and off she went. Well, say, I think we were all surprised to see it work, and it never worked better. There was almost an absolute calm all day, but we made good speed towards Portland. While passing Seguin Light, our experience of the year before occurred to us. We ran through the same squall in which some students from Bowdoinham College lost their lives. We could see the squall coming up and had got the sail off and stowed snugly some time before the squall struck. Then starting the engine we made our course by Fuller's Rock. We were a mile off Seguin with plenty of sea room, so I didn't worry. The engine kept pounding away and there was only a moment when her head fell off. When the squall struck, it shut in with thick rain and we couldn't see ahead of the bowsprit. It certainly blew like blazes for a few minutes, and the crew slid down on the cockpit floor to avoid being blown overboard. I presume we might have been making two miles an hour, and when it cleared we hadn't made any appreciable distance. I remember after arriving in Portland we had many inquiries regarding other boats, but I believe they were all accounted for but the sloop in which the students were sailing.

We arrived in Portland about 5 o'clock, anchoring off Peak's Island. Peak's Island is a general rendezvous for visiting yachts and we found the Lucy here and of course paid a neighborly call. Now, the Lucy is hospitable to a very sudden and frequent extent, and any refusal would cause distress, consequently we added to our interior decorations, and presently voted that life was not without its compensations.

In the evening we went ashore and the boys ran across some aquaintances, so that we had a very pleasant time and the party were invited to sail with us next day.

The next morning somewhere around half past one the boys woke the skipper up and wanted to get up and clean ship, but the skipper persuaded them with determination in his face and a windless stick in his fist, that while cleanliness might be next to godliness, he, the skipper, needed his beauty sleep, and he didn't think the yacht was as dirty as all that. However, the boys were uneasy and moaned in their sleep so that about 6 o'clock the skipper yelled, "all hands on deck." Well, they washed down the sides and then proceeded to scrub all the paint off the deck.

Looking Down From the Masthead. (Penobscot Bay).

About 9 o'clock, the ladies showed up, and of course in the inevitable white dress, and they looked real cute and pretty. Now, I don't know whether the boys didn't do their work well, but you would make no mistake guessing which part of those white dresses was used the most when they went home.

After awhile we got under way with a light breeze, and had a very good sail among the islands in Casco Bay.

Of course the ladies poked their pretty noses into most everything, and into some things they weren't supposed to. When lunch time arrived and coffee from the galley stove was served they thought it was "real cute."

Now it doesn't take very long to tell about a day's sail, and the small events which happen are very interesting when they do happen, but sound very tame on paper. However we had, as the ladies expressed it "a beautiful sail," and when back at the anchorage, with a full moon looking down, you can't blame the boys for hitching up closer to the ladies so their voices would blend better. Now, on the trip down, the boys had been bargain hunting and Paul had picked up a mandolin which he said he could play some and Toddy had bought an accordion, which he said he could play a little, and, if you'll take the skipper's word for it, he could play it a little, damned little. However, the skipper with banjo and Paul with mandolin, after some practice, could strike an occasional note together; however pretty bad music sounds good on the water, and time passes pretty quick when you are enjoying yourself. Eleven o'clock came so quick everyone was surprised, and when we took the ladies ashore they said they had a "lovely, lovely time," and they said it as though they meant it, any way we believed them, because we had had a pretty good time ourselves.

The next day dawned very smoky, but we got underway, with no wind. Ran with power out of the harbor, when a little breeze springing up we set sail and drifted along. Now, a light head wind doesn't mean much of a day's run, consequently it was well along in the afternoon when we reached Biddeford and anchored below the entrance to the Pool. The anchoring ground in the Pool is pretty small, and is all taken up by local fishing boats, so that visitors had better anchor below, where there is shelter from most winds. The harbor is not a particularly good one, neither is there much of interest in the place. The next morning we got underway again and sailed for the Isles of Shoals, which we reached soon after noon, Most yachtsmen have visited the Isles of Shoals, but they are usually given the go-bye. The government has recently constructed a breakwater, shutting off the easterly winds and making a pretty good harbor except in northwesterly high winds.

These islands have quite an interesting history. About everyone has read of and almost forgotten the horrible murder which was committed here. During the revolution, these islands were inhabited by a gang of practical freebooters who gave the authorities a great deal of trouble before they were finally dislodged. The islands are practically barren rocks, some of them of considerable extent. The inhabitants live on the proceeds of fishing. We went ashore in the afternoon and walked around. There are some places where the water has washed out and dislodged the rocks, forming places into which the sea heaves even in a dead calm, making quite an inspiring sight.

After getting back to the boat the boys went fishing, and we soon had a good mess for supper. These deep sea fish are hard and sweet, and when slapped into the pan as soon as caught are mighty nice. We got acquainted with a fisherman who, after the usual formalities, gave us some lobsters.

The next morning looked like a blow from the north and we thought we had better take advantage of it, so got underway early, having breakfast while under sail. The breeze was a fair one, driving us some five knots an hour. After sunrise, conditions looked more promising for a fair day. We arrived in Gloucester early, having passed inside the breakwater and between Milk Island and the mainland. Anchoring off the Clubhouse, we had dinner and went ashore in the afternoon. There is a very sightly trolley ride from Gloucester through Pigeon Cove and around the shore, taking in a great many bits of the rocky shore and then swinging around through Annisquam.

In the evening we took in a show and on the way back to the landing the boys found some blue jackets who wanted to get back to their ship. Now six huskies in a small tender don't allow much leeway for a sea, but luckily for us the bay was very calm, so we landed our freight O. K. and then rowed back to our own ship. In finishing up a cruise, most everyone likes a good day, so we were pleased when the next day proved fair and we got underway with a light wind, making fairly good progress with sheets lifted.

The skipper was reminded of his unfinished yarn on the run home, and commenced thusly:

"I believe we left the tired crew sleeping the sleep of tired mariners. Well, they were tired enough to stay in Portland the next day, but the day following was a smoky day, the wind being southwest, and we started slowly out of Portland. Setting topsails, we beat slowly along for some time. The breeze got better after a time, however, but as the sea came up with it, we were soon having a hard thrash to windward. We stood close inshore to avoid the sea as much as possible. The wind kept increasing and we were soon jumping into it, the yacht riding up on one wave and fairly diving into the next. We finally had to shorten sail, and along towards night reefed her down and set the storm jib. Billy and I took watches, I the first and Billy the last, each of us sleeping on the old jib in the standing room. It was an uncomfortable night for everybody, and hot meals were out of the question. Well, the night finally wore away, and in the morning both the wind and the sea went down. We had stood offshore in the night and found ourselves southeast of the Isles of Shoals. It was still so rough that all we could get for breakfast was some cold beans. The day was so smoky that we didn't sight land until about 4 o'clock in the afternoon, and it was about 8 o'clock in the evening when we drifted into Gloucester, where the skipper immediately went ashore to lay in something for a good hot supper, and for the next day. The run home the next day was uneventful and about the same as we are taking today."

I can't close this story without telling of an occurrence which happened some weeks after we got home. I tell it partly because it shows how easily and unexpectedly trouble can happen even with a crew more or less used to the unexpected. I also have in mind that my crew had sand in their makeup and the good judgment to use it quickly at the proper time.

On this Sunday of which I speak, we had the old crowd and their wives and sweethearts. We had been down the harbor in the usual way. It had been a nice day, sunshiny, a light breeze which had died out to almost nothing on the way home, making power necessary. We had got up to and passed Governor's Island, when we noticed a rowboat with a number of girls in it. They were making motions, but as there were a good many campers on the island, we took them to be over-exuberant campers and nobody paid much attention to them. Well, as we got along they paddled close to us and suddenly threw the painter of their boat to us. Hutch, who was forward, grabbed the line and took a turn around the starboard stay. The skipper threw off his power, letting the yacht slow up until the rowboat was astern, when the power was put on again.

Just what happened after this nobody knows, but it looks as if the painter of the rowboat broke, and the yacht's tender rode over her, capsizing her and throwing the seven girls into the water. For a second we were all paralyzed, but Hutch, taking in that someone was going to be drowned, dove over and swam towards the girls, the two Nutters following, while the skipper turned the boat around and nosed her up as near as possible. Two of the girls had grabbed the yacht's tender as she rode over them, and climbed in. One of the girls in the water, a plucky girl who kept her head and could swim, refused the aid of the boys, directing them to the girls who couldn't swim. By this time the yacht's head was close to them and the girls were all got aboard and their boat picked up. No one was much the worse for the wetting, although the girls were a somewhat scared lot, as they might well be.

A Summer's Cruise in 1911.

CRUISE OF 1911.

Since the foregoing was written and sent to press, another cruise of two weeks was taken, in the summer of 1911, and this cruise, as with every other cruise, has events and happenings all its own. Some new places were visited, and enough little things happened, so that the skipper feels impelled to add a few words more. He would have preferred to incorporate it in that already written, but so much had already been printed that it was not feasible; a small account, therefore, is the only alternative.

This had been one of those summers where everything was uncertain up to the last minute. Nobody seemed to know for a certainty whether they could get away, but get away we did, finally. The crew this year consisted of Bernard Lee, Connie Fish and his son, the skipper making the fourth member of the crew. Saturday night found all the crew assembled at the club, and all busy lugging aboard the multitude of articles always taken on a cruise. The tank was filled with water, the gasoline tank filled, the ice chest variously stocked with eatables, drinkables, etc; rigging was overhauled, spare anchors put aboard, the compass adjusted and many other things of more or less importance were attended to. The provisions had to be bought and got aboard, and when everything was done and stowed so that we could all get aboard and lay down, the whole crew was mighty tired, and nobody was at all fussy as to whether we got an early start or not.

We got under way Sunday morning about 9.30, after a good breakfast. The wind was fairly light from the South, but afterwards changed and blew from the Southeast, accompanied by a considerable sea. We had an average run to Gloucester. Everybody was tired and were glad to be out in the air and lay around. Lunch time came and went with only mild interest. When well along towards Gloucester, we were passed by a small motor boat, which stopped after passing us, and we afterwards heard that they were compelled to hoist a piece of canvas and run in behind the breakwater at Gloucester.

Monday morning was foggy, so we stayed in port, Nobody, I think, was at all sorry to have a day of complete laziness, and we all laid around and read, occasionally moving to consult the doctor or purser. Lunch seemed to attract more attention today. A visit to town in the evening gave us a chance to stretch our legs. After a walk around, we finally went back to the boat, and, as it was rather damp from the fog, the blankets felt pretty comfortable.

Tuesday morning proved a calm morning, the wind being southwest.

After breakfast we got under way and ran out by the breakwater; the wind was fairly light, but we got along fairly well. There was a considerable swell from the east, so, as the tide was low, we took the course outside of Milk and Thatcher's islands. After passing the Londoner, the breeze stiffened and we steadily increased our speed. We ran through the Isles of Shoals about 2 o'clock, making York River in good season for supper. Picked out our usual anchoring place. Got in our ice and supplies, had supper, and went ashore in the evening, taking a ride up to York Beach, where we moseyed around for a time and rolled a few balls at the pins.

It was pretty cold on the cars coming home, enough so to create an appetite, and after getting aboard, a small bite and a reference to the ice chest were in order before turning in.

The next morning dawned clear and bright, so after breakfast we got under way. The wind was fair, and we made fairly good progress until we got to Portland Head Light, when we started the motor, as it was getting late. After clearing up and snugging everything down, we went ashore and had supper and then wandered around awhile before going aboard again. The next day was spent in Portland, the skipper having small necessary repairs to the engine, and one of the boys also having a friend to look up. We went out to Cape Cottage to dinner, where Connie joined us with the information that the friend had been gone a week. After idling over our dinner awhile, we went back to town and walked around, finally going back to the boat and motoring over to Peak's island. The boys played ball awhile, and we all went to the theater in the evening,

The next morning proved fine, and we got underway for Bibber's island, where Connie had another friend summering. Bibber's island is about 15 or 20 miles up Casco Bay, from Portland, and it is a very pretty sail among the islands.. One has to be careful of his navigation in Casco Bay, as there are many shoals that have been built up by the ebb and flow of the tides, and there are also many reefs and isolated rocks that would easily pick up the unwary even in fair weather, while in a fog, discretion would lead the uninitiated to drop anchor and wait for fair weather. We had a good breeze and arrived in good season at the island. Connie went ashore to see his friends, while the rest of us idled in the cockpit, reading and smoking. There is no special harbor here and one would probably get considerable roll in a blow from the southeast. The bottom seems to be good hard mud, and there would be no trouble in holding on. The anchorage would be partially protected by a reef of rocks on the easterly side.

Connie came aboard after awhile with the information that his friends had been "gone a week." Say, this remark, "been gone a week," is getting monotonous, and the skipper is getting somewhat fearsome that his friend whom he intends to visit may perpetrate the same thing.

We stayed at Bibber's Island two days, meeting a number of acquaintances of Connie's, one of whom was known to the skipper, and who took us around in his launch.

Bibber's island is a pretty, well wooded island, rocky, and with some elevations. It is small and is fairly well covered with the usual summer cottages. It is small, an hour's leisurely walk encircling it. A steamer touches at the northerly end daily. Bibber's island is pretty much like the other thousand islands in Casco Bay and the storekeeper is like the rest of them, affable, and one who can name high prices just as easy, oh, so easy, just as though they were used to it. We bought, among other things, a blueberry pie. Now that blueberry pie was a good pie, a devilish good pie,—that is, it was when we started back to the boat; we paid 50 cents for it, so we kind of treasured that pie. We delivered the pie into Connie's hands for safe keeping. Now Connie is a mechanician, so we had a right to expect him to be exact in his movements. After leaving the road for the path leading down to the wharf where we landed Connie slipped on some hubble. It was a dark night but against the starlit sky we could see Connie execute a Siwash war dance, and it was a good one. He did his best and he lit on,—well, never mind about that,—it is sufficient to say that when he lit the upper part of him resembled the statue of liberty with the substitution of blueberry pie for the torch. Well, when later we had that pie, it was somewhat cracked and mixed, as though it might have passed through the San Francisco earthquake or something like that, but there was plenty of evidence left that it had originally been built along the lines of a good pie.

This day had been foggy, but the next was nice and clear. However, the boys had got some acquainted with, — well, it's none of your business if it was ladies,— so we stayed another day and enjoyed ourselves; we fished, swum, dug clams, etc., and, well, we did some visiting, too. We were ashore that afternoon when a sudden shower drove us to shelter, where we enjoyed ourselves for a couple of hours. We went aboard later and had supper, and naturally it was properly reinforced after the strenuous exertions of the day. The steamer coming along about this time, we pelted the crew with cold bottles.

After supper, we saw signs of a double cross in the southwest, so decided to sail the next day.

The morning broke good with a light southerly air, and we beat down the bay among the islands,— another pretty sail,—and out into the open, where we got more wind and bowled along in fine style past Seguin and up the Sheepscot River. The wind had lightened up some by this time, and we sailed past Hendrick's Head light, and finally dropped anchor on the easterly side of Boston Island. After furling up, the skipper went ashore, fearing to hear that remark, "been gone a week." The fates were propitious, however, and we found our friend at home. For the next two days it blew from the southwest, raining at times the first day. Bert had two motor boats, so between our loafing spells, we had trips in one or the other of them. The trip through to Boothbay was new and novel to the boys, and the trip up to Bath was pretty much the same, although more impressive. The next day, we took a trip up the Sheepscot to Wiscasset, a pretty old fashioned town, rich in historical events. The tide is pretty swift here and should be reckoned with in coming up here. We passed the old powder and block houses,—built in Indian times. They are well preserved, and it is to be hoped they will continue to be, as such relics are getting pretty scarce. The Sheepscot River is a deep stream its whole length, and large vessels come up to Wiscasset to load. We started back to Boston Island about five and reached home about nine. Through the kindness and hospitality of our friends, the boys had slept ashore the night before and this night also, and I know enjoyed the chance to run around. The next morning we were sailing for home, as our time is getting short; Bert and his boy are joining us for the sail to Portland.

The next morning we were up early, everybody busy getting things ready, but it was rather late when we got away. The wind was somewhat light from the south, and beating was somewhat slow work, so started the engine and ran it until by Fuller's Rock. The wind had increased, and we were soon having a hurry-up sail, close hauled, and jumping into a hard sea. Later in the day, we were able to slack sheets a little and made better weather of it. Ran into Portland about six o'clock, going ashore for supper. Strayed around town for awhile, getting back to boat about 11 o'clock.

The next morning being fine, we sailed towards home. The wind was light, so we ran the motor all day, and finally ran into Cape Porpoise about 5 o'clock. Had hoped to make York River.

The next morning the skipper had intended to start early, but on sticking his nose out at 4 o'clock, found the wind northeast, and a storm brewing. We made preparations to ride out the storm, putting out an extra anchor. The wind commenced to rise later, and it was soon blowing hard and raining. Three of the boats in the harbor left for home, two of them, however, found harbor further on, and one, the sloop Hilda, kept on, and later in the day was wrecked on the bar at Essex River. The skipper had a friend on a sloop which left York River that morning for home. They were caught in the blow off the Isles of Shoals, and ran before it with jib until it was blown away, when they put on the staysail. They pulled the stem out of their tender and lost it. Their captain showed excellent judgment in standing outside of everything off Cape Ann, as the rain made any observation uncertain. After rounding the Cape they stood in and finally picked up Halfway rock, and with this for a departure made Bass Point and Shirley Gut, luffing up when through the Gut and dropping anchor.

The skipper wants to say here, that, in his opinion, only the excellent seamanship and good judgment of the captain ever brought this sloop through what was a mighty hard blow, and he also feels as though he would like to take an axe to those inconsiderate,— well, what shall we call them?— (individual is weak, but it will have to go),—inconsiderate individuals, then, damn 'em, who suddenly get tired of being cramped up on a boat, and find that they have to be home a couple of days sooner than they had originally intended. In the case of the above sloop, I understand that one or two were in a hurry, and, of course, the captain felt impelled to sail, perhaps against his better judgment.

Saturday afternoon we got underway with the power, and ran to York River. There was a pretty bad roll from the storm and nobody enjoyed the run very much.

Sunday was a nice light day, and we ran with the motor in almost a flat calm, reaching Gloucester about 5 o'clock.

Monday morning was a repetition of Sunday, with a little more wind, perhaps, and we ended our cruise in an uneventful manner. Selah.

www.ingramcontent.com/pod-product-compliance
Lightning Source LLC
Chambersburg PA
CBHW030124240426
43673CB00041B/1390